To Phyllis

From Becky

Date Sept. 29, 2017

HIS EYE
IS ON THE
SPARROW

Artwork by
LINDA MARON

HARVEST HOUSE PUBLISHERS
EUGENE, OREGON

His Eye Is on the Sparrow

Artwork copyright © by Linda Maron, licensed by Creatif Licensing Corp.

Text copyright © 2013 by Harvest House Publishers. Original text by Peggy Wright.

Published by Harvest House Publishers

Eugene, Oregon 97402

www.harvesthousepublishers.com

ISBN 978-0-7369-5272-9

Design and production by Dugan Design Group, Bloomington, Minnesota

...and I know He watches me.

Always
Remember...

See
your own
beauty.

Magnolia grandiflora.

You Are Treasured

You are worth more
than many sparrows.

MATTHEW 10:31

*D*iscover the delight of knowing how much God cares for you. Allow this sweet and grace-filled truth to stir your heart. Be still. Listen. Do you hear it? It's your soul responding with expressions of gratitude, a melody of hope, and a tempo born of peace. This is your song. Sing it often and be joyfully blessed all the days of your life.

I sing because I'm happy,
I sing because I'm free,
for His eye is on the sparrow,
and I know He watches me.

A grateful
thought
toward
heaven is of
itself
a prayer.

GOTTHOLD LESSING

Put together all the tenderest love you know of, the deepest you have ever felt, and the strongest that has ever been poured out upon you, and heap upon it all the love of all the loving human hearts in the world, and then multiply it by infinity, and you will begin, perhaps, to have some faint glimpse of what the love of God is.

HANNAH WHITALL SMITH

Gratitude is not only the memory but the homage of the heart—rendered to God for His goodness.

NATHANIEL PARKER WILLIS

Remember that what you believe will depend very much on what you are.

NOAH PORTER

Excellent things are rare.

PLATO

The very word "God" suggests care, kindness, goodness; and the idea of God in his infinity is infinite care, infinite kindness, infinite goodness. We give God the name of good; it is only by shortening it that it becomes God.

HENRY WARD BEECHER

Kindness

is something we receive
and have to pass along
in order to keep it.

If one draw near
Unto God—with praise and prayer—
Half a cubit, God will go
Twenty leagues to meet him so.

SIR EDWIN ARNOLD

Oh, God, how beautiful the thought,
How merciful the blest decree,
That grace can always be found when sought,
And nought shut out the soul from thee.

ELIZA COOK

God loves each of us as if there were only one of us.

SAINT AUGUSTINE

Take time to
laugh
for it is the
music
OF THE SOUL.

Change

ALWAYS

COMES

BEARING

GIFTS.

You Are Blessed

My heart leaps for joy,
and with my song I praise him.

PSALM 28:7

When your voice grows soft and the demands of the day silence your melody, rest a moment. Be assured that your Creator is near. You are a blessed woman with a deep well of strength within a prayer's reach. With your tender heart renewed, your song will resonate with a new depth— profound and even more beautiful.

Why should I feel discouraged,
why should the shadows come,
why should my heart be lonely,
and long for Heav'n and home...

We love music for the buried hopes, the garnered memories, the tender feelings it can summon at a touch.

Letitia Elizabeth Landon

Between the humble and contrite heart and the majesty of heaven there are no barriers; the only password is prayer.

Hosea Ballou

Life is a gift of nature

beautiful living is the

gift of wisdom.

*T*he Lord my pasture shall prepare,
　　And feed me with a shepherd's care;
His presence shall my wants supply,
　　And guard me with a watchful eye.

JOSEPH ADDISON

A loving heart is the beginning of all knowledge.

THOMAS CARLYLE

Blessed is the influence of one true, loving
human soul on another.

GEORGE ELIOT

In all ranks of life the human heart yearns for the
beautiful; and the beautiful things that God makes
are his gift to all alike.

HARRIET BEECHER STOWE

Where mercy, love,
and pity dwell, there God is dwelling too.

WILLIAM BLAKE

Being deeply loved by someone gives you strength,
while loving someone deeply gives you courage.

LAO TZU

Such songs have power to quiet
The restless pulse of care,
And come like the benediction
That follows after prayer.

HENRY WADSWORTH LONGFELLOW

Love does not dominate;
it cultivates.

JOHANN WOLFGANG VON GOETHE

HARMONIA RURAL[

OR,

AN ESSAY

TOWARDS

A NATURAL HISTORY

OF

TISH SONG BIRDS

GURES, THE SIZE OF LIFE, OF THE BIRDS, MALE AND FE
IN THEIR MOST NATURAL ATTITUDES ;

HEIR NESTS AND EGGS, &c.

BY

JAMES BOLTON.

You Are Loved

*See what great love the Father has
lavished on us, that we should be called
children of God! And that is what we are!*

1 JOHN 3:1

Open your eyes as you hum your song and
see who gathers near. Friends—long standing
and newfound. Family—young, old, and in between.
They come because they love you. Leaning in, they
carefully listen for the tone that says you are well.
And then each steps near to lend their voice to
yours—and a sacred chorus of love fills the heavens.

*When Jesus is my portion?
My constant friend is He.*

21

When I hear music,
I fear no danger. I am invulnerable. I see no foe.
I am related to the earliest times, and to the latest.

HENRY DAVID THOREAU

Walk boldly and wisely...there is a hand
above will help thee on.

PHILIP JAMES BAILEY

God's goodness hath been great to thee:
Let never day nor night unhallow'd pass,
But still remember what the Lord hath done.

WILLIAM SHAKESPEARE

If you would
be loved, love and
be lovable.

BENJAMIN FRANKLIN

The divine essence itself
is love
and wisdom.

EMANUEL SWEDENBORG

Sing again, with your dear
voice revealing
a tone
of some world far from ours,
where music and moonlight
and feeling
are one.

PERCY BYSSHE SHELLEY

Kindness gives birth
to kindness.

SOPHOCLES

Have you had a kindness shown?
Pass it on;
'Twas not given for thee alone,
Pass it on;
Let it travel down the years,
Let it wipe another's tears,
'Til in Heaven the deed appears—
Pass it on.

REVEREND HENRY BURTON

Angels descending, bring from above,
Echoes of mercy, whispers of love.

FANNY J. CROSBY

When Christ ascended
Triumphantly from star to star
He left the gates of Heaven ajar.

HENRY WADSWORTH LONGFELLOW

His eye is
on the sparrow,
and I know
He watches me.

You Have Assurance

I call out to the LORD, and he answers
me from his holy mountain.

*A*re you curious about the divine? Embark
on a personal journey to discover truth—
rock-solid and eternal. By faith step into the
loving presence of God and open your tender
heart to the Teacher. Find your voice and ask your
questions. It's okay. He's been waiting for you...
listening to your song, once tentative and hushed,
now brave and strong.

"Let not your heart be troubled,"
His tender word I hear,
and resting on His goodness,
I lose my doubts and fears.

He leadeth me, O blessed thought,
O words with heavenly comfort fraught,
Whate'er I do, where'er I be,
Still 'tis God's hand that leadeth me.

JOSEPH HENRY GILMORE

Wonder is the desire for knowledge.

SAINT THOMAS AQUINAS

God writes the gospel not
in the Bible alone,
but on trees and flowers
and clouds and stars.

MARTIN LUTHER

Be assured, if you
walk with Him and look to Him, and expect
help from Him, He will never fail you.

GEORGE MUELLER

Prayer is the voice of faith.

RICHARD HENRY HORNE

He who, from zone to zone,
Guides through the boundless sky thy certain flight,
In the long way that I must tread alone,
Will lead my steps aright.

WILLIAM CULLEN BRYANT

There they stand, the innumerable stars,
shining in order like a living hymn, written in light.

NATHANIEL PARKER WILLIS

Cherish
YESTERDAY

Dream
TOMORROW

Live
FOR TODAY

Oh, the comfort, the inexpressible
comfort of feeling safe with a person, having
neither to weigh thoughts nor measure words,
but pouring them all right out, just as they are,
chaff and grain together.

DINAH MULOCK CRAIK

Just as there comes a warm sunbeam into every
cottage window, so comes a love-beam of God's
care and pity for every separate need.

NATHANIEL HAWTHORNE

The soul can split the sky in two and let the face
of God shine through.

EDNA ST. VINCENT MILLAY

You Are Confident

He put a new song in my mouth,
a hymn of praise to our God.

PSALM 40:3

O n the mornings when the sun is shining bright
and your heart is free from anxious thoughts,
loosen your tight grip on an expected life and
dare to celebrate the day. Unfurl your closely held
dreams to the Spirit. Revel in the freedom and give
in to pure joy. Sing out confidently for you are a
beautiful creation, favored and beloved!

*Though by the path He leadeth,
but one step I may see.*

39

Grace comes into the soul,
as the morning sun into the world;
first a dawning; then a light; and
at last the sun in his full and
excellent brightness.

THOMAS ADAMS

When the green woods laugh
with the voice of joy,
and the dimpling stream runs laughing by;
when the air does laugh
with our merry wit,
and the green hill laughs
with the noise of it.

LORD BYRON

40

Don't trust to
hold God's hand; let Him hold yours.
Let Him do the holding, and you the trusting.

HAMMER WILLIAM WEBB-PEPLOE

He enjoys much who is thankful for little: a grateful
mind is both a great and a happy mind.

THOMAS SECKER

Faith is to believe what we do not see; and the reward
of this faith is to see what we believe.

SAINT AUGUSTINE

Scatter joy.

RALPH WALDO EMERSON

The windows of my soul I throw
Wide open to the sun.

JOHN GREENLEAF WHITTIER

Who brought me hither
Will bring me hence;
No other Guide I seek.

JOHN MILTON

Without faith a man can
do nothing; with it all things
are possible.

SIR WILLIAM OSLER

delights them ... I think before
this flower ... others deserves
beauties ... the stately aspect and
... colors ...
... matched or
garden for th
... Tulipas an
his flowers or ... others
... delight ... so ...
... a ...
... be ...
... and ...
... and ...
... color ...

*His eye is on
the sparrow,
and I know He
watches me.*

You Have Hope

By day the LORD directs his love,
at night his song is with me.

PSALM 42:8

Every now and then you might feel as though your sweet melody requires too much effort. The notes seem long and the tune difficult to carry. Do not despair. You have a faithful Friend who sees your struggle and understands your concern. Your strength will be restored in His presence. And you will be given a new song that fills your heart with gladness and your spirit with enduring hope.

Whenever I am tempted, whenever clouds arise,
when songs give place to sighing,
when hope within me dies...

Hope is like the wings
of an angel, soaring up to
heaven, and bearing our
prayers to the throne of God.

JEREMY TAYLOR

Three grand essentials to
happiness in this life are
something to do, something to love,
and something to hope for.

JOSEPH ADDISON

Hope, like the gleaming
taper's light,
adorns and cheers our way.

OLIVER GOLDSMITH

Every heart that has beat
strongly and cheerfully
has left a hopeful impulse
behind it in the world, and bettered
the tradition of mankind.

ROBERT LOUIS STEVENSON

God sent his Singers upon earth
With songs of sadness and of mirth,
That they might touch the hearts of men,
And bring them back to heaven again.

HENRY WADSWORTH LONGFELLOW

I see heaven's glories
shine and
faith shines equal.

EMILY BRONTË

*H*ope is that thing with feathers that perches in the soul and sings the tune without the words and never stops...at all.

EMILY DICKINSON

Live
the LIFE
you've
imagined.

Hope is like the sun, which, as we journey toward it, casts the shadow of our burden behind us.

SAMUEL SMILES

There is no medicine like hope, no incentive so great, and no tonic so powerful as expectation of something better tomorrow.

ORISON SWETT MARDEN

Hope is the dream of a soul awake.

FRENCH PROVERB

Far away there in the sunshine are my highest aspirations. I may not reach them, but I can look up and see their beauty, believe in them, and try to follow where they lead.

LOUISA MAY ALCOTT

You Are at Peace

Peace be with you!

JOHN 20:21

s your journey continues, so does your song—adapting and adjusting to the cadence of your life. Though the verses are endless, speaking of spectacular events, exceptional people, and beautiful ideas, your chorus is the foundation. It's what you've come to believe—to know as truth...*I sing because I'm happy, I sing because I'm free, For His eye is on the sparrow, and I know He watches me.*

I draw the closer to Him, from care He sets me free.

First keep the peace within
yourself, then you can also bring peace
to others.

THOMAS À KEMPIS

When I look like this into the blue sky, it seems
so deep, so peaceful, so full of a mysterious
tenderness, that I could lie for centuries and
wait for the dawning of the face of God out of the
awful loving-kindness.

GEORGE MacDONALD

The feeling remains that God is on the journey, too.

TERESA OF AVILA

POSTE ITALIANE

SMILE

BREATHE

AND

GO SLOWLY

LONDON

*M*ercy among the virtues is like the moon among the stars, not so sparkling and vivid as many, but dispensing a calm radiance that hallows the whole.

EDWIN HUBBEL CHAPIN

Best of all is it to preserve everything in a pure, still heart, and let there be for every pulse a thanksgiving, and for every breath a song.

CONRAD GESNER

Speak, move, act in peace, as if you were in prayer. In truth, this is prayer.

FRANÇOIS DE FÉNELON

There is radiance and
glory in the darkness could we
but see—and to see
we have only to look.

Friar Giovanni Giocondo

It is not how much we have,
but how much we enjoy,
that makes happiness.

Charles Spurgeon

Contentment opens the source
of every joy.

James Beattie

Go on
with a spirit
that fears
nothing!

HOMER

His Eye Is on the Sparrow

Lyrics by Civilla D. Martin, Music by Charles H. Gabriel

Why should I feel discouraged,
  why should the shadows come,
Why should my heart be lonely,
  and long for Heav'n and home,
When Jesus is my portion?
  My constant friend is He:
His eye is on the sparrow,
  and I know He watches me;
His eye is on the sparrow,
  and I know He watches me.

Refrain
I sing because I'm happy,
  I sing because I'm free,
For His eye is on the sparrow,
  And I know He watches me.

"Let not your heart be troubled,"
  His tender word I hear,
And resting on His goodness,
  I lose my doubts and fears;
Though by the path He leadeth,
  but one step I may see;
His eye is on the sparrow,
  and I know He watches me;
His eye is on the sparrow,
  and I know He watches me.

(Refrain)

Whenever I am tempted,
  whenever clouds arise,
When songs give place to sighing,
  when hope within me dies,
I draw the closer to Him,
  from care He sets me free;
His eye is on the sparrow,
  and I know He watches me;
His eye is on the sparrow,
  and I know He watches me.